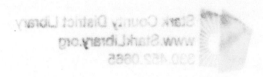

Table of Contents

Rourke
Educational Media
rourkeeducationalmedia.com

Can you find these words?

dinosaur

fossils

measure

skull

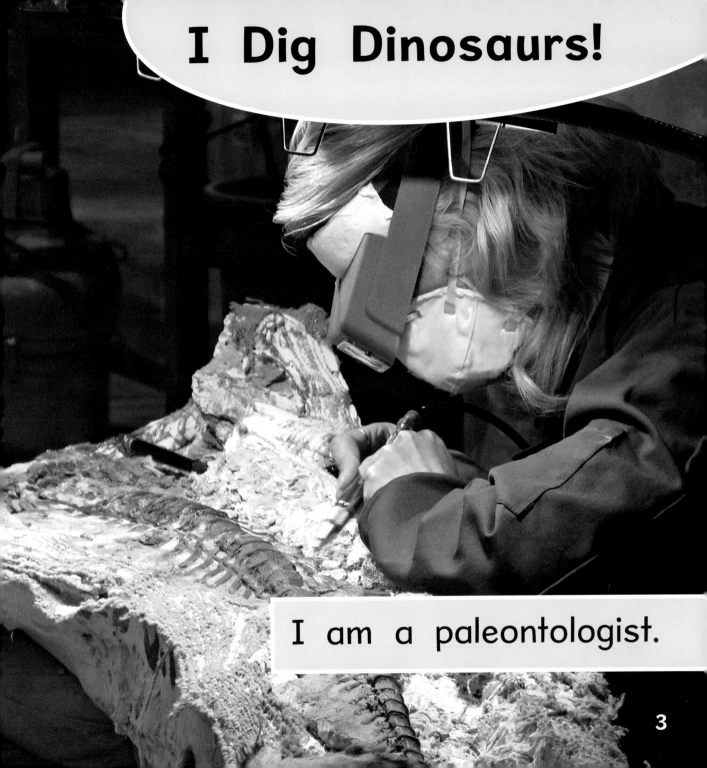

I Dig Dinosaurs!

I am a paleontologist.

I search for **dinosaur** bones.

dinosaur

fossils

The bones are called **fossils**.

When I find bones, I dig them up!

Clunk goes my shovel.
Tap goes my hammer.

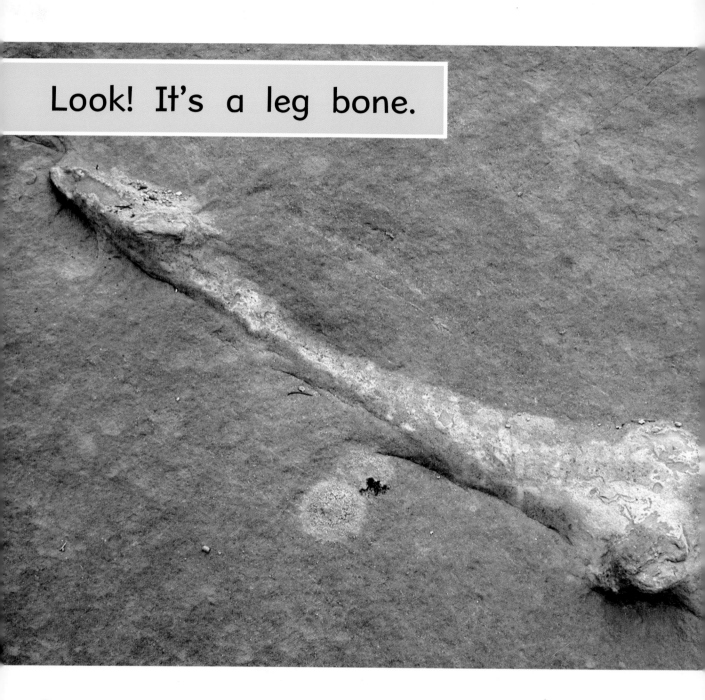

Look! It's a leg bone.

There is a giant **skull**, too!

skull

I **measure.**
I draw.

measure

I take pictures.

11

Studying dinosaur bones
is a BIG job.

But it's the job for me!

Did you find these words?

I search for **dinosaur** bones.

The bones are called **fossils**.

I **measure**.

There is a giant **skull**, too!

Photo Glossary

 **dinosaur** (DYE-nuh-sor): A large reptile that lived in prehistoric times.

 **fossils** (FAH-suhls): Bones or shells from animals that lived millions of years ago.

 **measure** (MEZH-ur): To find out the weight or size of something.

 **skull** (skuhl): The bony frame of the head that protects the brain.

Index

About the Author

Katy Duffield is an author who lives in Florida. She has a husband and a dog. But she doesn't have any dinosaurs. If she could have a dinosaur, she would want a Triceratops.

www.rourkeeducationalmedia.com

PHOTO CREDITS: Cover ©DavidHCoder, Page 3 ©benedek, Page 2,4,14,15 ©JonathanLesage, Page 2,5,14,15,©Snowshill, Page 6 ©tacojim, Page 7 ©Jim Gibson / Alamy Stock Photo, Page 8 ©Mistercheezit, Page 2,9,14,15 ©BertBeekmans, Page 2,10,14,15 ©microgen, Page 11©wanderluster, Page 12 ©PhotoScape, Page 13 ©Peter Casolino / Alamy Stock Photo

Edited by: Keli Sipperley
Cover design by: Kathy Walsh
Interior design by: Kathy Walsh

Library of Congress PCN Data
I Dig Dinosaurs / Katy Duffield
(Let's Find Out)
ISBN (hard cover)(alk. paper) 978-1-64156-192-1
ISBN (soft cover) 978-1-64156-248-5
ISBN (e-Book) 978-1-64156-298-0
Library of Congress Control Number: 2017957802

Printed in the United States of America, North Mankato, Minnesota